Haste

Poems by
Lisa Bickmore

SIGNATURE BOOKS | 2023 | SALT LAKE CITY

But how late to be regretting all this, even bearing in mind
That all regret is late, too late!

—John Ashbery

www.signaturebooks.com

Photo of author on back cover by David Hyams.

SECOND EDITION | 2023

Library of Congress Cataloging-in-Publication Data

Bickmore, Lisa Orme
    Haste : poems / by Lisa Orme Bickmore.
    p. cm.
    ISBN 1-56085-061-2
    I. Title.
    PS3552.I318H37   1994
    811'.54—dc20   94-31753
                                         CIP

Second edition ISBN: 978-1-56085-465-4
Ebook ISBN: 978-1-56085-482-1

Contents

Foreword

It's at least a little disorienting to look back at work accomplished half a lifetime ago—in the case of the poems in *HASTE*, quite literally so. These are the poems I wrote as a poet coming into her own. These are poems that came out of my dreams and out of the grit of my life as a young mother and wife. I still dream in poems, and some of my poems still come from those years, but in my waking life, my beautiful children are grown, there are cherished grandchildren—many of them—and I am closer to the end of my life now than to the beginning.

I'm so grateful to Signature Books and its editorial team for publishing *HASTE* in the first place, and for reprinting it now. I'm grateful to the writers I studied with—Bruce Jorgensen, Larry Levis, Richard Howard, and (briefly) Mark Strand—for everything I learned from them about writing poems and a life in poetry. I'm grateful, also, to friends who read these poems, and to classmates in writing workshops, who were the friends of these poems as they found their better forms.

I heard the poet Tarfia Faizullah say once that poetry is an ancient form of storytelling. In this collection, I wanted to tell my own stories, but also connect them to the stories that mattered to me—of my neighbors and friends, of the scriptural and mythological lore of a culture, of a life that I, along with others, was dreaming and hoping into being. I wanted to find my own place in that ancient storytelling art. I believe I began to do that in *HASTE*. I thank these poems for finding me, and helping me to become a poet in the writing of them. And I'm so glad to be able to share this book again with readers—I hope they find surprise and pleasure here.

Lisa Bickmore
December 2, 2022

Small Fires

The Dream-Work

The figures have less to do with recovery
than with resistance: not going to the garden
in October to gather the dry cornstalks,

not the flare of lights in the kitchen
at five. Not the expected spiders
in all the corners after first cold,

not the snow line descending nearer
the valley, or the scarred, crewcut hills.
What we recover every autumn, each withered

garden, the same sinking light every year.
Each night they seem this familiar,
but they resist capture or even

clear sight: looking through the window,
steamy from the warm house and the dishwater,
waiting for father, seeing only the diffuse

headlights turning. Looking into the face
of a man I loved once, now gradually
not his face but someone else's, this man

I knew once, in a silk suit, saying,
It's what you want, you want this—yes,
but what is it, exactly? Its name transparent

and relentless, a current of air or water.
His name—he doesn't matter, he's here to ask
about desire, what I want: alone on the late

street, him shoving me against the wall,
saying, *you want this*; fearful I won't
escape this desire, or that I will.

Hastening

The oldest poem:
Its verses recursive in these scenes:
The big tableau, Vegas at sunset,

and vast clouds complicate the sky,
their fat forms clotted with pink light,
rose paint suffusing the Dunes' neon palms.

And they roll on, faster and darker, and
the gamblers do not recognize the night.
North, at home, the cold comes back; but

on the Strip, I am not there to see
the cold-slowed roses loosening one sepal
each day, the impatient frost on the grass.

In the restaurant at morning the smell
of coffee and bacon, and in the next room
the gamblers drink Bloody Marys—they

haven't yet slept. And at home, the baby
holds on to a chair, then lets go—stands
balancing, his first steps nascent in his stance.

The Suicides

They knew the others would find them after the fact
with their reasons clutched in their hands,

or folded into a pocket. They knew, too,
that the others had heard them, in their flat sentences,

saying, How difficult things had become.
How hard it was to fail. How strange it was to be

no one, and yet how loud the noise
that persisted in their heads. That the others

had ignored them, or heard them, and moved on.
And if they had thought of it, they would have imagined

what the others were left with: fragments and pieces.
The terror of cleaning up, the labor of guilt:

turning, seeing the houses burning, a heap of ash,
the windows that framed the world in glittering

shards, the jagged formations of salt. Everything
and nothing. The rope, the gun, the flame.

They walk unfalteringly into a room
where the others are not permitted,

not looking back, closing the door, locking it
as tight as a knot. The room empty and full.

The souls moving like insistent whispers.
This is how the others imagine them—a chance, an insinuation—

since the door is locked, the walls opaque as flame.
They have walked alone and away.

Straight Way Out

Have meditated upon it since the night at the amusement park
when I heard of your death by fire, your own hand
striking the match.

Melodrama's one thing, and deliberation another, but on the lawn
you flickered between them: a simple self-consuming act;
a gesture of decision

That I admire very much, even if it is not my way. Imagining this life
as a room, and one way out through the door, if the room is only
minimally cluttered;

Or if in the presence of a single heat, what to one might seem
an insurmountable accumulation might simply evanesce, evaporate,
become the ghost of that life

that is to another as palpable as a body one longs to touch.
And one does not step over or step through
that loved body or even

that body's shadow. One picks one's patient way around
the circuits of that life, the room of which begins to seem a whole
world, with a door or window

that hold themselves open with the idea of openness,
toward which one never seems to make one's way. . . . I have tried
to understand the suicides,

their impatience—the press they make for that open door—
and despite the stolid doggedness that keeps me wending
my way around this room,

and the temptation, as of a body one longs to touch, of their swift
unheeding feet: the room itself begins to change
and the clutter grows roots

and becomes something green—a potted fern, maybe even an ash
tree, a sapling, but with flowers unlike anything natural—
flowers the color of flame.

Elegy for a Housewife

for Sabra

The cold locks in like a coffin in this valley.
Some Januaries it drifts in of an afternoon,
When the winter sun is still clear, rebounding
From snowbank to snowbank, blinding
And bright—then the fog makes its soft entrance,
A bolt of sheer fabric draped over the houses and streets,

A January extended to the indefinite. You didn't
Last long enough to see it this winter.
Before it ever set its tentative foot on the field
Outside your door, the way the snow lay, gray
And threaded with the wild grasses, the stones
In their old places, veiled with the snow,

And even that worn with the pattern
Of the persistent wind: this seemed so familiar,
So that even a wide-windowed house would not ward off
That wearing and sighing that carved out cliffs
And hollows in winter's face. Driving home last night
In the fog, watching the tail lights of cars

Ahead of me as they vanished, the lights themselves
A kind of blindness, gathering all the mist to them—
The lines on the road made the only flat sense in what seemed
An apotheosis of incandescence. The lights are all like that—
Following in sequence, bursting past me on familiar roads
That I don't recognize. The fog makes them an aurora,

A lower northern lights—red, yellow, green, and white.
What is missing is the blue, and for that we have to wait
Till morning, or till the morning that breaks in a few weeks.
Just this week, we had an afternoon hazy with sunshine,
That watery winter light bitter and brittle
With cold. I know, you have refused all this, you who used

To refuse nothing. But the air, filled with a dust of diamonds,
The drifting particles made crystalline, was enough
To make us believe that the air is a presence, our true
Element. By ten days you missed it, by just days,
The air's diamond dust drifting down to earth, our mortal dwelling,
The house you turned from, the rooms you inhabit no longer.

Doomed, Sick, Selfish, Dumb as Shit

In those days, my first behind a camera, I used black
And white, a more intelligent medium than color,
Whose glassy brilliance obscured every moody
Shadow of my vision. And thus
This photograph of two babies,
One with her hands clasped confidingly, and a wicked grin;

The other at six months ready to fly,
Or fly apart, the hands in their splayed
Disorganization, mouth pursed to hold
His lifted head up, his balance on the stomach.
Somewhere in the background there, in what
The drape covers, one imagines it waiting—

Black and white admitted that shadow, that germ of decay,
Without my knowing. But open the drape, and in it spills,
The clotted gold of the sun, and all the gaudy colors pursuant.
It is the raucous artistry of this world to work
In color, the whole palette expanded to include
The red skull cap on the head of this street mother waiting

With her makeshift family and their grime at the bus stop,
Their private laughter in a public space tinted
And divided into the spectrum of a rainbow, which
Swirls on the iridescent lenses of this young girl's
Sunglasses, holding her baby in his carseat as she
Raises her voice to speak over the loud beat of

Her friend's boom box outside the mall.
Out of those speakers emerges a music as big as all
Ambition, as big and as richly hued as the once
Eminent and estimable glory of the self, sad specimens
Of which we see around us always and everywhere.
Confess a certain gladness at its visible decline—

Like the gritty effacement of the high monuments,
The way this world moves at a certain time of day
Toward the limited range of a gray spectrum, and how
We may predict with more solid evidence that indeed
Nobody loves us all, or anyway, not enough—hence
The fear inherent in cities, neighborhoods, walls

And locks. But this evident indifference allows us
Our nostalgias, which is why I return again
And again to this photograph, black and white, the two
Lives there at their beginnings, in the pristine moment
Before the inevitable spill and stain of the world's eloquent
Colors, the consequent beginning of memorials, and decay.

The Glad Quality of the Things Beneath the Sky

These bright things exist in our world
Despite the condition of loss,
Which, by fiat, governs all
—or so I thought, looking around:

The sad houses that need paint, long roads
Adorned by nothing but the hum
Of wires and a broken painted line;
The way even miraculous birth

May be marred by accident and defect.
The autistic boy at the bus stop, his dance
Of rocking back and forth, the rhythmic
Shift of his wide stance—I cannot help

But stare, such movement superfluous
To bus stops. He knows this, knows his excess,
And stops when he sees me; but it resumes,
His dance, as soon as I look away.

It is unembellished, a simple step of forward
And back, the repetition the entire point;
And my gaze only a segment of the strand
Along which embarrassment, acknowledgement,

And gladness are strung. Before loss,
The very stones learned to sing; one imagines
With the proper teacher, they might also
Have learned to dance. I used to think

That the point of all this was beauty, that
The stones sang in voices drawn
From mineral throats, inhuman and like
That fabled harmony of the spheres.

Perhaps I have always been wrong, and the glad
Song of the stones made beauty beside the point:
Much else in our world escapes the logic
Of beauty, and only the moment of loss

Forces us to elide the sheen of gladness resting
On things. Perhaps that rocky song emerged
Scraping along from granite throats, off key
And maybe even without rhythm. Orpheus

Possibly found that once he'd taught them,
He couldn't stand it, all the earthly
Things singing in their flat tones, their
Inharmonious keening, sucking the breath out

Of the world that, in its silence, had once
Seemed pregnant with song. Perhaps Orpheus,
Contrary to legend, even welcomed loss,
Embracing it with tears streaming down

His face, beauty following hard on the retreating
Figure of Eurydice. Melodious songs of exquisite
Grief are the legacy of that moment; I still
Can't escape a tear, the luxury of a sob,

When I hear them: but I like also
To witness the way things evade the elegant
Patterns of their designs: windows lined
With foil; the blinds at other windows

Warping their horizontal planes, inclining
Toward the center of each blade; how these blinds
Still raise each morning to admit light, and in
Contrary motion, at the end of day, lower to contain it.

Reconnaissance

1.

We knew the nights he flew high and hunted, but where
His plane searched, and for what, was his secret.
For freedom, I thought then, and later, for the war,
Its names and places reasons for his absence: Da Nang,
and the Gulf of Tonkin, Tet, Hanoi and Saigon.

His absences I remember, but rarely his returns,
Only coming home from school, the house breathing with
The exhaustion of his sleep. How little I know of his life.
We drove past the hangars once, and he pointed to the big
Belly of the C-130, for him humming with intelligence.

I imagine him now high over the South China Sea, approaching
The central highlands, the fat curve of the coast, heading
South toward the delta of the Mekong, or north to Da Nang—
I search the map of Southeast Asia, and find no names to tell
Where he went, for how long, or how far. So I suspend him

In flight over the South China Sea, at indeterminable height
Headed somewhere, toward the strange place where strange people
Waited for him, at an unlocatable distance from us, alive
In the cockpit, reading the complicated pattern of lights,
The instruments that guide him where he flies.

2.

Waiting for war and bad news: it was the story
Of my mother's life, the three years we lived
In Japan, in our little house built where the rice
Had once grown. Three children and the thin walls,
And the wind roaring around us while the rain
Pelted the roof. We sat round the table all night,
The candles dripping wax to the wood while we waited
For the typhoon to end, for father to come home.

How available she was to us: her face open to loss
Even as she tried to seal it, keeping the candles
Lit like a prayer. And still I know where to find her:
In that desire for return, the talent for holding the lives
Of children and men close, while all around her, people
Were leaving, climbing into the cockpits of planes,
taking off into the sky. She waited, her patience
The still point. Her face open to this absence, this return.

3.

Always returning, sometimes to the picture
Of the small girl in the dress and blue hat,
The hat not hers but her father's,
With its silver braid and the eagle.
In other pictures she wears hose and heels,
Her mother's, with similar glee. Or surely
I must have, in pictures I remember, or imagine—

But I do not return to these pictures.
Instead I come back to a geometry lesson,
The serious inking of proofs,
My father's way with a pencil on graph paper,
The theorems falling so finally into sense.
Just as finally, my mind consents to that logic,
To the order my father composes

Of the Greek for Euclid's elegant
Regular forms. By then it had become a pattern,
The insistent return to this man, my father,
Finding him beside the lemon tree where he
Had mounted a telescope over the back fence,
The mirror he himself had polished enclosing
The stars the way the rings encircle Saturn.

At midnight he could map that corner of the sky
That they inhabited, as dark as all space,
As busy and as empty. If he'd turn the telescope
On me, its concave mirror fixing the image,
Perhaps he could as plainly map the way
I came to be this kind of woman, his daughter,
Invent the proper instruments for finding a father, a mother.

16

Black Ice

We might still drive on, sideways, sliding
To the muddy edge, the wind and ice

Locking our wheels into wreckage.
We do not drive without heading straight

Toward that moment: the black sheen of ice,
The wind's whine, bring us closer, impose

The pulse of danger, danger. It has been
An eternity of cold, and still I remember

The time the windshield cracked, its frame
Emptying gems as we sprawled in the postures

Of the helpless. We counted the injuries
And the losses, emerged stunned but whole.

The bruises of hip and thigh have faded,
No trace or mark. That afternoon, safe

In the car of strangers, I found imbedded
In my finger a seed of glass, its sign no more

Than a pindot, the only blood I saw. If anything,
It is this that, somewhere inside, glitters black.

Extravagance

All this week they have fluttered in the stiff May wind,
These tiny painted butterflies, who've travelled,
We read, from Mexico, where lived so many of them
That these had to go. It's hard to imagine what would be
Too many butterflies, when here drift thousands across

The western-most road; when the reticulated triangles
Of broken wings litter the walks; when I find one,
Spent, exhausted, on my lap as I drive, the merest
Quiver of silk to indicate a shred of life. It does not
Matter, the idea of excess, to those that alight

On this spring's exuberance of dandelions.
The formula (worked in insect algebra, one guesses)
That separates *enough* butterflies from *too many* has been
Worked months ago in northern Mexico; these, the remainder,
Followed northerly currents to arrive in a place

Nearly too cold. Cold enough, at any rate, even in May,
To halt the migration. If, as we've also read, this is travel
Which includes no return trip, we are, for this moment,
Allowed to register the air, alive now as in autumn
With fragments of brittle color; to notice how our steps

Cause a thrill, the beating of innumerable tiny wings;
To remark the specimens our children bring to us;
To imagine that we, like emperors, walk on paths
Awash in silken wings; to begin again to define *too much*
In a world composed on the principles of extravagance.

Maple Seeds

The big maple limbs in the gutters lie so heavy
The stormwater's rush downhill cannot move them,
So heavy we imagine them not cut by the city's
Tree trimmers, but broken from the trees by the wind
And the May snow that folds the leaves on themselves

In their glazed coats. All week, though, spring renovation
Goes on in the storm, crews at the crossing shoring up
Embankments, the lights alternating warning and the bells
Banging, the long light of the train moving slowly over
The tracks past the fixed red semaphore. In the afternoon,

An interval of sun, when the crews take off their jackets,
And the steam rises from the flanks of horses, the dirt
Of their corrals, the just-plowed fields. By our house,
The Queen of the Night tulips bend, black, their heads
Beaten down. But before the storm moves on, spring's

Green detritus collects under the trees, the broken leaves
Sailing in the swift gutter, the tiny maple seeds
Green as pairs of mantis wings. The larger ones
Clinging to the trees will stay there for summer, wait
For a different, drier wind to take them whirring in their flight.

The Mind Turns to Its Own Figurations

It costs me exactly nothing,
That handful of coins,
Yielding its slight but not unaccountable
Weight into her hand, her pocket.
I leave what my mother used to call
Folding money folded inside,
And barely break stride.

The Navajo woman blesses me,
Asks God to bless me,
Declares the Lord will bless me.
Money, like metaphor, feels neutral,
And changes hands cleanly,
Its clinking music cooling the skin
That holds it, then gives it up.

I've been told that God hears
The supplications of all the ones crying
God bless you on behalf of those
Who help the poor beggars of this world,
And I've no doubt that the Mother
Theresas, saints of slums, will roll
In heavenly bank accounts,

That accumulation of figurative gold.
Who'd begrudge such hypothetical
Capital? As for me and my flippancy,
We walk lightly on, the spring air
Showering down its ancient currency,
Invisible coins, with complex
Inscriptions, as if newly minted.

Surrender

At the end of each broken day, stepping with bare feet
On the stale crumbs of our brittle day's bread,
I vow to stem my longing for what I can't have:

The unmarking of my body, a fatal elegance,
True love with a stranger, God's face, a sure sign.
I pray instead for the ordinary, the daily,

The miraculous banal: crumbling soil, sweet pea vines
Climbing the iris swords, a quiet house at five
In the morning, the chiaroscuro clouds. If I

Cannot love these, I ask then for a slow-paced heart
To move me in an even beat, not in this contredanse
I do with desire. Before the break of dawn I wake

To the hum of dream machinery, the hollow inside
Pulling matter and marrow to make a hungry core:
And even before I rise I whirl on the axis of desire.

The Road Out of Lewiston

At the point the horizon erases what we can see
I think the road must rise into the sky, invisible,
Circling back to where it began, wherever it began.

This Doors tape, an endless loop droning ahead
To the start, from Riders on the Storm to L.A.
Woman—each time it clicks over, I say to myself,

The beginning. Like this trip to Los Angeles—the origin
Is no place until the return, when I say, *where I started.*
That boy sitting on the margin of the freeway,

With the cardboard sign and his thumb—he is
Returning, or leaving, one can't tell from his
Position there his place on the circuit

Of travel. Now he waits on the road out of Lewiston,
Past the confluence of the Snake and the Clearwater,
And I see him near the ledge banked sharp

Against the sky, a curve so fast and so high,
I think, if the guardrail gives, I'll swing out wide,
Break into an open blue ascent.

Putting Away the Year

October, the end of the warm duration, & autumn's rain
Has begun to wash the color from the last zinnias. The roses unfold
More slowly now than in August, when they opened & shed

Their petals in a day. October's end surprised us
This year: the summer spilled past its boundaries into
September, the weeks warm with a season lasting past

Its moment. This day, the sky pulled closer with the cold,
Cloaking us in a fall of gray rain, we bend to uproot
The plants from their beds, finding the dirt again crumbling

From the spent roots, & and the drying water-spotted leaves.
The perennials stay—gypsophila, dianthus, gloriosa,
Lavender & carnation. The tall cosmos still bloom, so we relent

& allow the open flowers, the curled buds, to wait for the frost
That withers and blackens. The spent roses we break from the canes,
& the hips that gather their black seed. The petals

Of the roses, the zinnias, calendulas, marigolds, we break
Apart into the earth, uncovered again, doing its good work
Of making & unmaking in the last of this year's garden.

Night's Last Child

for Jim and Tina Currier

In the summers we used to play at night until
The moon was high over us and the sky had filled

With stars: then we all went in, slamming screen
Doors behind us. And collapsing into beds,

Still sweaty, we fell into sleep, as if sleep
Had found us in the last game of hide and seek.

In that neighborhood, the mothers trusted us
To each other: and we had each other to find

When we were hiding. The same kids in my
Neighborhood now: and as nights get longer,

And the smaller ones disappear into houses,
Older kids remain, their hair and skin sweaty

And warm, down to the last kid alone in the evening.
I see them riding bikes home at ten o'clock;

The same kids who walk the railroad tracks,
Steps slow, measuring the ties; slow, and as straight

As the path a boy ran in the last field
Of winter wheat, a lonely and breathless passage.

Small Fires

We waited in a hot wind for the storm
To lift the current up from the close-nubbed field,
The summer the lightning lived in our hills.
We waited on our porches for the spectacle
Stinging close to the huddled houses,
Close enough to charge our own street:
We felt it in the dangerous rattle of windows,
In the kindling of the soles of our feet.
The day late July it leapt to the roof
The hot white flower trembled there in the wind,
And we lived at that moment for the heat in the bloom,
That small flicker at roof's pitch,
And the low sky storming with light.

I have imagined it possible to collect such days,
Such light, and though I have not since
Been taken by light of that candor, no other day
Has opened so wide a color: now the nimbus
Accumulates over canyons, the cleaved foothills
Fill with shadow, repel the day's last light.

And if I have imagined such possession,
In the lengthening wait between days
Winter blackens the hours by five,
And at seven already the light
Pools in the bowl of the valley;
And I run in darkness and wrench
My ankle in an invisible hole, and pass
Under the only streetlight which
Flickers and recedes from me.
These moments remind me that every day
Spends its lingering light in darkening
And that nothing is mine: not the summer fire
That woke me from a heavy sleep, not smoke
So close it seemed to curtain the hills into
Rooms I might enter, walk among;
Not even the mottled medallion hanging flat
Over the Oquirrhs, the moon
I run toward breathing
Hard in my lungs, though already
It is fading into the fading blue.

What to Pray for

Once I folded hands and said the old words,
So intimate, except in speaking to God,
A conversation that turned them into gems,
Hard and colorless. If now I recall the posture,

It is the same motion that causes me
To collect words for prayer: the word itself
Gathers the associations of hours
Spent on knees talking to bedsheets and

Listening for voices, hands clenched in one fist.
Hearing instead the speech of heartbeat, of
Breath in and breath out, the stroke
Of the slow blood swimming back to the left side.

At night I might still kneel, hear that wordless
Reiteration; but always I make words
For the things I pray for: the empty spaces on maps,
Envelopes postmarked Huntsville or Fairbanks,

A letter with a ptarmigan feather in it,
And the story of the dull bird careening flat
Into the window of a friend's house.
For the flat planes of the mountain mined

Open, oxidizing into the colors of copper,
And the gathering of water into rivers,
The spilling of spring floods. For the opening
Of doors in summer, the dust accumulating

Quietly on the piano. For the ripening and rotting
Of apricots, a night without sleep,
A morning too early. For the intelligence
Of the body even in decay, fingers that turn

The tap in exact calibrations to water the lawn.
For the thickening of breast and belly, a name
For the coming child, and these words of prayer
That sing all night in my veins.

Love's Body

Happiness

for Abigail

As if it were a reward, somehow, for hope—
It is a useless idea. You find it somewhere
Along the arc that begins at expectation, that
Disappointment ends. If you were to predict

A point on that arc at which it would be likely
To occur, it probably would not be in bed
On a snowy morning, with the milkman's footsteps
Printed on the walk, then turning away; with

The tousled sheets just warm on your legs, your body
Deciding whether to relax into sleep, or gather
To rise; the baby's head turned away from you;
Her every breath under the quilts lifting them

With a shudder, then a sigh. Who would ever dream
Such a moment as one particularly happy?

Elements

for Steve

Before we went to sleep,
We huddled on the floor,
Searching an old map of Utah,

Seeking the legend of those
Dry dusty names, austere mysteries
We've never seen: Cataract Canyon,

The Needles, Standing Rocks,
The Windows, the Maze. Then,
We fell to the desert of sleep,

Dreaming separate dreams of red
Rock, hot stone, God's arches
Sculpted from the strata

Of time, and the sand,
Shards of that hard light

Then I found
Myself awake, naked as stone,
Your lips at my breast;

But before I wholly woke,
I half-dreamed myself part
Of the red dusty hills,

That elemental, with the purest,
Deepest groundwaters running
Secret in me, deeper than you

Or anyone could plumb,
Deeper even than the most ardent
Well of love or desire.

Love's Body

for Amelia

i.

It is very small. It emerges with no language.
It is itself a language. It exits me, squalling;
Its inscriptions read, *firstborn daughter*.

ii.

We hold her and study her. She sleeps solemnly.
Her skull is shaped with a delicate chevron
Placed precisely, its opening saying, *brain*; the
Point saying, *eyes, the view*.

iii.

We clothe her in tiny garments that obscure
The unbearable detail of her anatomy. The sleeves
Of her gown, for instance, envelop her fingers,
Since the nails may mark her face. The fine
Bones of those fingers, the pink nails like fragments
Of beach shells, are so miraculous we must cover them:
We can bear only a glance.

iv.

In the rituals of cleanliness we observe,
I realize that I cannot trust
The world into which she must grow. I wash her,
Take clean white diapers brought punctually
Each week by a clean white van, swaddle
Her buttocks, abdomen, genitals, mute with wonder
That I cannot make a world in which water
And white gauze are sufficient protection.

v.

I imagine this body grown woman-size, opening
Her self to the uses of sex: I imagine first
A gentle partner, one who loves her body as much
As I do, I who brought her body here—then
I turn away from the hard man
Who is indifferent to her, who makes her
Fit him, who changes her always. I do
Not want to see if their faces are different
Or the same.

vi.

I remember her back before, before
She emerged, her inarticulate voice,
When she was still a little lodger, my body
An efficient hotel. She checked out
After her last month's rent was paid up.
How quickly the staff cleaned up after—
The blood, the milk drying up—
And we stand, two female bodies,
The imprint of the one on the other almost
Invisible, like a newly made bed with clean sheets.

My Discontent

In the night we sleep in endless dialogue,
And if a child creeps between us, our bodies
Wake to argue as if our voices had never ceased,
As if we never slowed a breath or word.

In a twisted nightgown I lie awake after sleep
Takes him, put my arms around him, listen
To his breath's cadence. The child sleeping
Between us, her hair smells of white soap,

I stroke it with my right hand; the left under
The pillow like a slice of dreamer's wedding cake
I might wish upon, dream endlessly of endless
Marriage. One man, one mind. I carry

The girl back to her bed, my shadow moving
Before me on the wall washed in white
Midnight. No child between us. In the dark
I make my way back to my discontent,

To him sleeping, as if sleep might close something;
Me waiting to ease into a less interrupted sleep.

Abandonment

The breath of my children hovers over their beds
Still and unwavering, nothing disturbing

The field of their sleep. The spotted dog
Sprawls on the floor among discarded garments,

A moan in his throat as he shifts his great bones.
I imagine them leaving one by one, before

They're ready, stepping with that grown assurance
Of a fortune to be made, but with the height and posture

Of an eight, a six, a four year old, their baby sister
Creeping behind. Or they leave all together: no longer mine,

Refusing to cohere as mine, their faces blank, staring
Past me, not recognizing in my face the face of their mother.

And so it must have been me: I must be the one leaving,
I walk away and don't look back, so that they lose my face

In the crowd of souls walking away from one another, leaving
Choirs of dogs behind them as they go. Or I turn a key

To fire up the car with one speed and no brakes,
The engine of this dreadful plot in which I find a room

Where the bathroom is white, the surfaces clean:
And if I return . . . and when I return, to the house I left,

And there is no one there, and I have no address: do I go on
To live in that deprivation, the absolute free exile?

A Woman in Her Thirties

stays awake after   the household is blanketed
in sleep   for late silence is the best silence
and an awaited solitude   as sweet as wine

uncrosses her legs   and stands to cross a room
looks at the man she knows   or doesn't know
and says   *why him?*   and then   *why not?*

dreams dreams that freight   her daily steps
with faces and gestures   she wants to handle
with a grave hand   a lingering touch

smells the heaped pears   in the basket
and touches the table   bearing them up
the scent of onion   staining her skin

knows the music of the voices   that inhabit
her house   its transient phrases and melodies
hears the ghostly episodes   when the house empties

can lay and light the fire   that flickers before
the altar of preservation   that saintly incense
the smoky flame proclaiming   both *hearth* and *burning*

in any case

If there is any sense to be made of this at all,
it will be in the insistence of the lower case—the diminutive
letter—an envoi in miniature, never sent.

It must be diminished, because this figure
looms so large, so lifelike, in dreams—eyes
a golden hazel, the fiber of the coat making

its rough impress. And the license the appearance
of that figure gives to lawlessness, criminal
behavior one wants to enact, but which one must let

fall, censored and uninscribed: this figure may not speak
its lively speech. In effect you must be scribe and translator
of what lives in the wide space between desire and act:

mute love and speech: allowing the silence of the former
its powerful moment, the full round minute before declaration.

Sleepwalking

for Lilas

I run water into the green cup, and my son
Drinks, then pads down the dark stairs
To his bed where he will dream deep
Till morning. Nights like these I walk back

To bed with eyes still closed, though I only
Float the surface of that shallow stream
And wait for the next small body standing
Next to me to pull mine out. She wakes

To tell me the terrible story she has invented
With her eyes closed, that I must revise for her with
The curve of my body against hers in my bed. For
The smallest I find the lost blanket she has kicked

To the bottom of the bed where her feet do not reach.
I turn off the light, and turn it back on.
I hear their footsteps though they are sleeping.
Anyone who wants to can walk into this bedroom.

This night my old piano teacher walks in
In her nightgown to sit on the edge
Of my bed, crossed leg keeping time,
Pulling dark threads from a ravelling hem, but when

The clock digits click, she believes
The clench of my eyelids, the weight of my sleepy limbs.
And when his hot hands touch me, I turn
To my husband, but in his face move

The uneasy faces of a hundred men
Whose names I know and do not remember.
I get up and go to the window to see
The dark windows of houses before dawn,

The brightness of the white street.
Outside a pale peignoir hangs
Gracefully on the peach tree's lowest branch,
But I turn back to my bed through a crowd

Of moving murmuring bodies, whom I ask
To forgive me, it really is my bedtime.
They arrange themselves by ascending height,
Whispering stories that insinuate sleep.

In the Old Way

As in every summer of my younger, lesser life,
This July we went north to our cabin. More than the place
Made by the sturdy hands of my father, my grandfather,

More than a city-dweller's retreat, more even than
The story of wilderness and restoration, spring of the big West:
It seems at this point to be stored in my cells, the longing

For the long road through fields of wheat, barley, potatoes,
The georgian vistas of eastern Idaho. We stop
To get the key from my grandparents, have breakfast

Without haste around their table. It is a fast eighty miles, some
Of us dozing through Ashton and Sugar City, but when
We hit the trees and the altitude, the air is unmistakable:

As in every old story of clean air, we inhale as if starved,
Expanding our boundaries, exhaling what we've left behind.
We speed past the lodgepoles' insect-eaten, fallen, naked trunks

In horizontal disarray, and the new trees' green spikes
Piercing the debris. And when we get there, to the cabin,
The trees new just about fifteen years ago (a storm knocked down

All the old ones that summer), when we unlock the doors, enter—
The believers entered their shrines in this way, once, removing
Their shoes, raising the dipper of sacred water to their lips,

Rinsing their hands, shaking drops of light from their fingertips,
The rites of people at the thresholds of holy places.
We're people without such ceremonies, but as we bring our food

In from the van and put it on the shelves, with a wrench
Turning on the water and drinking the first cup, opening the windows
And lighting a fire, too warm even for a mountain night,

We can believe that we are celebrants of an ancient god,
One who intervenes favorably on our behalf, who gives us luck;
A fisherman's god who yields up trout from the rivers of the region;

A god of afternoon rain showers and warm enough nights;
Of skies blue in the morning and black at night, and filled
To the brim from his cup of stars; who lengthens and deepens

The calm spell of our sleep, and multiplies our pleasures
In love. A god of affection, and hence we are loath to leave
When we must, to sweep the floor and draw the curtains,

Shut off the water and lock the doors. Promising it won't be
So long till next we come. Driving away, the slow miles
Down the mountain, back to newer houses, their modern ways.

Corridor

for Sophie & Walker

She runs, her feet as intelligent as her hands, the ball
Moving with their quick pace. Behind her runs
Her brother, much smaller, and she knows he hopes
That he will get that ball, make it go far with the force
Of his little legs. It is late afternoon on a fine September day.

On one field her older brother plays with his team.
At the near edge, she could hear their hard breathing;
If she slowed, she'd see the flex of their muscles, smell
The sting of their sweat. On the other field are girls,
Like her, soccer players, but older, and they too breathe

Hard, sweat, run with the force of young bones strung
Like instruments with muscle. But for her their play
Recedes, their pale movements shifting with the whimsy
Of kaleidoscopes; her own movement in her own body
Runs west toward the sun at its western limit. She has made

Of the space between the two fields a green corridor,
Having as its origin the east where rose the sun this day,
As its terminus the west where now it sets. Behind her runs
A tiny boy, trusting her sure step, her feet with the rolling ball,
As they advance over the field's gentle curve toward the dark.

Late Winter Snow

All this long evening it has been snowing,
And before morning it will snow more:

It is midnight now, but the night sky is still cloaked
By the clouds, with their gray opaque light.

Before morning they will splinter into stars.
I stand at the window looking into the sky

And see the clouds begin to break into snow;
And I think of you, and of the street where

The houses end, where the big fields will fill
With snow. Before anyone wakes I will walk

The white streets, and walk past the houses,
Whose windows will still be dark, closed to me;

And the clouds will hold, close and gray, with no hint
Of sun, the light that would unlock this winter

Weather. And all through this night, still bright
With February snow, you will move through my sleep,

As long and as faithful as this weather
That I love, that I know can't last much longer.

The Swan Brothers

The Messenger

He was not asleep when I came to his camp.
Thinking about the droves of goats, no doubt,
The sheep, camels, cattle, and asses he had sent
To his brother, the gift preceding the bearer
To sweeten, he hoped, the bitter taste
Still lingering with the other over the business
Of the birthright, the pottage, the father's blessing.
He always was a clever man. The sleeping dogs
Stirred but didn't wake; and in the wind's drone
He did not hear me slide under the tent flaps.
I pinned him fast, an arm around his neck;
Another holding his elbows tight behind his back.

The hot fear heaved in his lungs, and he could not
Speak; but then the smart desert man's body
Began its twisting and slipping. He knew
All the ways to make himself awkward: and so
We wrestled there until the break of day,
When I cried, "Let me go, for God's sake!"

"Not until you bless me, whoever you are,
Coming into my tent and grappling with me till
The life's nearly gone and my thigh's out of joint!"

I'd wrestled his kind before, and pinned them flat,
I almost wanted to try again; but I had no more
Strength for wrestling. I could hear the women
Stirring in their tents; soon they'd be brewing
Their bitter tea to break the night's fast.
He told me his name after we broke apart,
I offered my blessing: I gave him the name
He asked for, the name whose long story would hold
Not only Abraham and Isaac, but among them
Reckon Leah, and Esau, the sons of Ishmael—
All the marginal ones, cast out, or lost,
Not favored.

                I left him there on the blankets,
His head cast down: he would break bread
With his wives, and then go to meet Esau,
Trembling, bearing the burden of God's name.
The brothers would embrace, Esau falling
On Israel's neck, kissing him, weeping.

In the Morning of Time

All the night before, my sleep was green,
Scented by the odor that by day
I smell everywhere, as bitter and as beautiful
As the light that opened me to the new world,
The world to its new brilliance.
I had not imagined it would be already
This riot of plant, this chaos heavy
With scent and seed and flower.
Now I spend my days with the spike-leaved
Dandelion, the yellow corona exploding
Into a haze of seed, and the twine
Of the morning glory, its mournful
Hearts for leaves, the pale ruffle of its flower.

That first day I didn't see their life
Underground, how I'd have to seize
The flat circles of leaves and twist till
The ground broke and gave up the root
Like a fat bleached carrot. Or how
The white morning glory root teemed
Without light, turning, turning, restless
To open into air, leaf, flower. We were
Once so sure that we could name
Plants and animals—one would sway in wind,
Another leap, or crawl; but now I am rooted
To this field, my hands green with the weeds,
And everywhere the roots, lithe
Underground. This was for our sake:

That the weeds break the earth,
Crumbling into this new life.

Immigrant

On this spring evening, Mr. Nguyen,
I watch you watching your sprinkler
Wreathing circles of sibilant rain in its orbit,
The necessary water for this dry country.
You saw me walking early in the twilight,
Smiled your broad grin to say hello;
It is as much as we can do. We do not speak
The same tongue, though we know enough
To pass as neighbors.

                              It is later now,
The moon not yet high enough to cast
Its sheen of light upon the lawn.
Though you can likely see me
Sitting here on my porch, watching
You and your water, you do not smile
This time, or wave. You are deep
In the orange tip of your cigarette,
Its slight curl of smoke. The country
You left was green, from leaf to stem
To ground—even the blackening light
Of the moon leaves the shimmer
Of the green patina. Here you must arrange
Your family to fit into the narrow shade
Of the summer's lone poplar tree,
Its leaves glittering in the afternoon sun.
In this dry country the green labors
For its place, it must be coaxed,
It must be fed the vital water.
It is a ritual you have been forced to learn,
The spring-and-summer tending of the dry
Earth; but now you are father of this lot
Of thirsty land, you smoke your cigarette
And let the smoke curl up,
The transient proprietary sign.

Francesca

". . . quel giorno piu non vi leggemo avante."
—Inferno V.138

In those days, *love, love, love* was all my song.
Now I speak to you, one of the dead, who cannot sing,

Except the thin thread of a cry rent, endlessly, from my throat.
In those days, when my love called me, softly, I would go,

My feet swift and light, the pulse fast in my veins.
How wonderful, the body so fleet, almost without weight:

And now, I long for that body, but slower, a steady hand
On the reins, and not this weightless whirling devil's dance.

Before we coupled, before desire seized us in its grip,
Before we secretly read the romance, the book in my lap,

His hand turning the pages . . . before all this, what was there?
I have forgotten, though memory's a curse here—

The moment, the moment, that was all we cared for, and it seemed
To last eternally, until the moment passed: then that fierce dream—

The longing for more moments. Fools that we were, we cast
Away the future as dross, and blotted out the past:

As lovers of a story, you'd think we'd not forget the strength
Of past, present, future, and the force of events that stretch

Along that passage. Here, of course, the moment *is* eternal.
In the book of life, we read birth and youth, then death, the diurnal

Round that predicts rise, glory, decline, and fall. Here the rule's
Desire and desire, the wind that propels the dance of love's fools.

The Snow Queen

1.

First of November, and an early snow. An eerie
Morning, the snow casting

Its alternate light, as if itself luminous.
Under a cold sky, I take the shears

To lop the last roses, the blooms edged in ice,
And I turn and almost see her, a near miss,

Since she had just left her cold signature.
Only two days ago all the flowers were singing

Their irrelevant songs: the blowsy cosmos, *I
Am tall, taller than all*; sweet pea vine, *I*

*Twine among the taller flowers, but my habit
Is fragrance*; calliopsis, *I am the sun, see*

My ragged rays. But she has made them
To lie down, their cacophonous chorus quieted.

One hears them, reclining, their faint narcissistic
Complaint. But the lips of the roses are frozen shut.

2.

I know the flowers don't sing, and yet, among words
Some of the most tuneful I know are names
For flowers. The boy and the girl thought so,

Under the verdure, the bower of roses under which
They sat, with their little book, naming the flora
And fauna of their beautiful world. The shard

Of ice that invaded his eye turned him from
Their green book to the hard face of a frozen woman:
Dante heard her too, in stony rhymes, that

Woman who makes men spell out
ETERNITY in fragments of ice. The girl wanted to stay
Under the roses, suffused with fragrance, and the light

That seeped down through the filter of leaves. But the ice
Had worked its way to the boy's heart now, so infatuated
He had become with the Snow Queen, and so the girl must go.

3.

Why must she go? The fragment
Was not hers, her eye remained

Uninfected, and she wanted to stay
There, with her book, the flowers,

That impossibly kind light—
But the boy had jeered at her,

And mocked their "nature" as
A book for girls. He preferred

His cold puzzle, assembling
And disassembling, while his

Heart froze and his hands
Darkened, blue with cold.

And the girl ran northward,
Barefoot, carrying the sympathetic sun

As if it were the very blood that hastened her
Onward, that blood that would heal him.

4.

My garden is not like the one in which Gerda tarried—
We are well past first frost, and it is too late

For tarrying, or for beginning any mission
Of rescue. I can almost imagine, or remember,

The full round day of summer: and then
I think I might be that girl, my garden

Emblem and effect of nature; that these
Flowers come up from under to redeem something,

To publish their idiot songs, noise their chorus
Of color. In November, how easy to dismiss that

Chorus, to forget how persuasive are color and song,
How they include one in wave on wave of

Opening and blooming and fading and dying.
In the palace of ice, that sympathetic garden

Must come to mean everything, figured so
Irresistibly as a girl whose tears and embrace

Might thaw the hard sky, yield the sun;
Might melt the coldest eternal prison.

5.

Tears and an embrace:
How these opened the pair
Back into the wide redeemed world
Where was no winter,

But only water and sun,

Where the roses sang an
Autonomous soothing song—
I am red, I am blood, I
Am nature, the feminine;

If I choose, I shall open

Myself and heal you—
As the boy became man,
The girl a woman, it was a song
Whose meaning was made plain.

The Swan Brothers

for Richard Howard

Some nights in bed, when no one needs my speech
Or listens, I remember myself, a girl
On the sand at sea's edge, and the first time
I saw them fly: birds at sunset falling
Toward me, white bodies in a free plummet,
The sun's swift slide racing to the horizon.

This was, I think, the best time for us—
For a moment simply eleven swans, then
The tall bodies of my eleven brothers,
Recognition and the clamor of family.
I woke from that dream with a nettle
In my hand, with silence my habit.

And my brothers watched me nights, crushing
Nettles to flax, spinning thread, weaving
Cloth. They too were silent, as if
They were voiceless birds still, and labor
Conversation enough. The youngest wept
On my hands and feet, blistered from gathering

And crushing nettles. My silence kept us
Each night, the lull of the wheel in our sleep,
Unbroken by any word. Morning woke me
To the rush of so many wings. I was not
Surprised by the king's coming—a neighbor—
Of course I went with him, and he would keep me:

To him I was mystery, woman weaving,
Woman without words. It was like that
At first, he would listen to the loom
Watching me as my brothers did, who now
Were flying everywhere; but my silence
Made him uneasy. So that when he saw me

Going nights to the churchyard to gather
Nettles, it was too much: when I returned
The still graves must have shadowed me, and
He turned away. I sewed the last shirt
In a mule-drawn cart on my way to be burned.
My hands stitched a straight sentence:

My brothers beat down around me, and I
Threw the shirts over the birds with a cry,
Making them into men. By now not used
To words, I fell faint, and they told my story.
My story: I live with it now as with a scar,
Another lasting estrangement, like the wing

Of my youngest brother, whose shirt had no
Left sleeve—there was no time to finish.
He has lived with me all the years since,
And we never speak of it, nor of why
I turn to him when we sit in silence,
As the night folds close to the windows.

The sea's heavings, before moonrise,
Remind me of my brothers' first falling
Toward me, toward where I always stood,
Arms open, calling to them; and of how
They fell to their sister, as if what I said,
Or failed to say, might save them.